Just Right Reading

Level A

Options Publishing Inc.

Level A

Acknowledgments

Product Development: The Quarasan Group, Inc.
Cover Design: The Quarasan Group, Inc.
Editor: Amy Gilbert
Production Supervisor: Sandy Batista

Credits   Abbreviations are as follows: t=top, c=center, b=bottom, l=left, r=right

Photos: Page 2 ©Corbis; 3 ©Corbis; 4 (t) ©Digital Vision/Punch Stock, (b) ©Michael Newman/PhotoEdit, Inc.; 18 (t) ©Michael Dwyer/Alamy Images, Ltd., (cr) ©Ambient Images Inc./Alamy Images, Ltd., (cl) ©Corbis, (l) ©Lee Snider/The Image Works, ©Eyewire/PhotoDisc, Inc./Punch Stock; 19 ©PhotoDisc, Inc.; 20 ©Andre Jenny/Alamy Images, Ltd.; 21 (b) ©Grace Davies/Omni-Photo Communications, (tr) ©PhotoDisc, Inc./Punch Stock; 22 ©Eyewire/Punch Stock; 27 (tl) ©Lee Snider/The Image Works, (bl) ©Corbis, (br) ©Ambient Images Inc./Alamy Images, Ltd., (tr) ©Eyewire/PhotoDisc, Inc./Punch Stock; 28 ©PhotoDisc, Inc.; 29 (l) ©Corbis, (cl) ©Eyewire/PhotoDisc, Inc./Punch Stock, (cr) ©Corbis, (r) ©James Watt/Animals Animals, (t) ©Digital Vision; 30 ©James Watt/Animals Animals; 31 ©Digital Vision/Punch Stock; 32 ©PhotoDisc, Inc.; 33 ©Tim Davis/Corbis; 34 ©Corbis; 38 (t) ©James Watt/Animals Animals, (tc) ©EyeWire/PhotoDisc, Inc./Punch Stock, (bc) ©Corbis, (b) ©Corbis; 39 ©Tim Davis/Corbis; 51 (t) ©Robert & Linda Mitchell/CritterPix, (l) ©Corbis, (cr) ©Stephen McDaniel, (r) ©Dorling Kindersley Picture Library, (cl) ©PhotoDisc, Inc./Punch Stock; 52 (t) ©PhotoDisc, Inc./Punch Stock, (b) ©Colin Keates/Dorling Kindersley Picture Library; 53 (t) ©Maria Zorn/Animals Animals, (b) ©Robert & Linda Mitchell/CritterPix; 54 ©Lynda Richardson/Corbis; 55 (b) ©Dorling Kindersley Picture Library, (t) ©Dorling Kindersley Picture Library; 60 (cl) ©Dorling Kindersley Picture Library, (cr) ©Stephen McDaniel, (b) ©Corbis, (t) ©PhotoDisc, Inc./Punch Stock; 61 ©Dorling Kindersley Picture Library; 73 (t) ©Lawrence Migdale, (cl) ©PhotoDisc, Inc./Punch Stock, (l) ©PhotoDisc, Inc., (r) ©PhotoDisc, Inc., (cr) ©Corbis/Punch Stock; 74 ©Mark Gibson/Index Stock Imagery; 75 ©Mark Gibson/Index Stock Imagery; 76 ©PhotoDisc, Inc./Punch Stock; 77 (t) ©Image Club Graphics, (b) ©Richard Hutcings/PhotoEdit, Inc.; 82 (l) ©PhotoDisc, Inc./Punch Stock, (cl) ©PhotoDisc, Inc., (cr) ©PhotoDisc, Inc., (r) ©Corbis/Punch Stock; 83 ©PhotoDisc, Inc./Punch Stock; 95 (cl) ©Michael Newman/PhotoEdit, Inc., (cr) ©Digital Vision/Punch Stock, (l) ©John Boykin/PhotoEdit, Inc., (r) ©Eric Fowke/PhotoEdit, Inc., (t) ©PhotoDisc, Inc./Punch Stock; 96 ©Mark Segal/Index Stock Imagery; 97 ©John Boykin/PhotoEdit, Inc.; 98 (t) ©Michael Newman/PhotoEdit, Inc., (b) ©PhotoEdit, Inc.; 99 ©Chuck Pefley/Alamy Images, Ltd.; 104 (bl) ©Digital Vision/Punch Stock; 105 ©Mark Segal/Index Stock Imagery; 121 (t) ©Michael Newman/PhotoEdit, Inc., (c) ©Robert & Linda Mitchell/CritterPix, (bike) ©PhotoDisc, Inc., (b) ©Corbis; 122 (t) ©Eyewire/PhotoDisc, Inc./Punch Stock, (b) ©Ambient Images, Inc./Alamy Images, Ltd.; 123 (t) ©Digital Vision/Punch Stock, (b) ©Corbis; 124 (t) ©PhotoDisc, Inc./Punch Stock, (c) ©Corbis/Punch Stock, (b) ©PhotoDisc, Inc./Punch Stock; 125 (t) ©Dorling Kindersley Picture Library, (c) ©Eric Fowke/PhotoEdit, Inc., (b) ©Corbis; 126 (t) ©PhotoDisc, Inc., (c) ©Lee Snider/The Image Works, (b) ©James Watt/Animals Animals; 127 (t) ©Stephen McDaniel, (b) ©Eyewire/PhotoDisc, Inc./Punch Stock; 128 ©John Boykin/PhotoEdit, Inc.

Illustrations: Dana Regan: 7, 8, 9, 10, 11, 13 Kris Dresen: 24, 25, 26 Fran Newman: 35, 36 Todd Bonita: 40, 41, 42, 43, 44, 46, 47, 48 Rita Lascaro: 56, 57, 58, 59 Marla Baggetta: 62, 63, 64, 65, 66, 68, 70 Shirley Beckes: 78, 79, 80, 81 Mike Reed: 84, 85, 86, 87, 88, 89, 90, 91 Paul and Alice Sharp: 101, 102, 103 Holly Hannon: 106, 107, 108, 109, 110, 111, 112, 113, 114

ISBN 1-59137-438-3

Options Publishing Inc.
P.O. Box 1749
Merrimack, NH 03054-1749
TOLL FREE: 800-782-7300 • TOLL FREE FAX: 866-424-4056

www.optionspublishing.com

Table of Contents

Table of Contents

Letter Review

▶ **Write the missing partner letters.**

A __   Bb   __c   Dd

E __   F __   G __ __h

__i   Jj   K __   L __

M __ __   __n   Oo   P __

Letter Review

▶ **Write the missing partner letters.**

‑‑‑‑‑‑ q   R ‑‑‑‑‑   S s   ‑‑‑‑‑‑‑ t

U ‑‑‑‑   ‑‑‑‑ v   W w   X ‑‑‑

Y ‑‑‑‑   ‑‑‑ z

Good work!

Get Ready to Read
A Day at the Park

1 Characters

Me

Sam

Mom

2 Setting

park

3 Words to Learn

run

play

climb

eat

4 Building Background

What can you do at a park?

A Day at the Park

We can **run** at the park.
I like to run.
Sam likes to run, too.

We can **play** ball at the park.
I like to play ball.
Sam likes to play ball, too.

We can **climb** at the park.
I like to climb.
Sam does not.

Wait!
I know what we both can do.
We can **eat** at the park.
I like to eat.
And Sam LOVES to eat!

Main Idea

▶ **What is the story about?**
Draw a picture.

Beginning Sounds

▶ **Circle the pictures whose names begin with the same sound.**

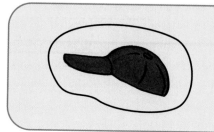  

1

2

3

4

Beginning Sounds

▶ Say the letters in the box. Name each picture. Write the letter that stands for the beginning sound.

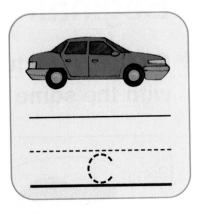

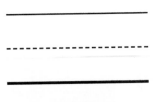

Beginning and Ending Sounds

▶ **Name each picture. Decide if the name begins or ends with the letter in the box. Write the letter on the correct line.**

c

_____ _____

- - - - - - - - - -

_____ _____

---

c

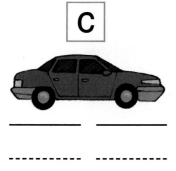

_____

- - - - - - - - - -

_____

t

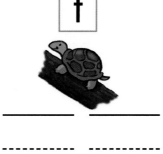

_____

- - - - - - - - - -

_____

p

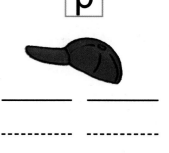

_____

- - - - - - - - - -

_____

---

p

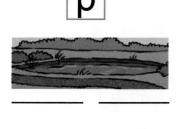

_____

- - - - - - - - - -

_____

t

_____

- - - - - - - - - -

_____

l

_____

- - - - - - - - - -

_____

---

c

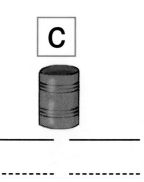

_____

- - - - - - - - - -

_____

l

_____

- - - - - - - - - -

_____

t

10

_____

- - - - - - - - - -

_____

Words to Learn

▶ **Write a word from the box to make each sentence tell about the picture.**

climb   eat   play   run

1 We can _____ .

2 We can _____ ball.

3 I can _____ .
Sam can not.

4 We both can _____ .

Read Aloud

▶ **Read sentences from the story. Take turns.**

Wait!

I know what we both can do.

We can eat at the park.

I like to eat.

And Sam LOVES to eat!

Share

▶ **Draw what you can do at a park.**

2

Get Ready to Read
In the City

1 Topic

a city

2 Words to Learn

people buildings cars bus

3 Building Background

What can you see in a city?

In the City

This is a city.
People work and play here.
They live here, too.

This is a busy city.
You can see many tall **buildings**.
You can see many **cars** and trucks.

There are many things to do
in the city.
You can ride on a **bus**.
You can play in the park.
You can go to a ball game.

There is a lot to see and do
in the city.
What would you like to see
in the city?
What would you like to do?

Details

▶ **Think about what you read. Draw a picture to show what you can see and do in the city.**

What You Can See

What You Can Do

Beginning Sounds

▶ Circle the pictures whose names begin
with the same sound.

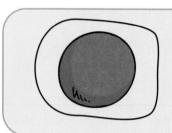  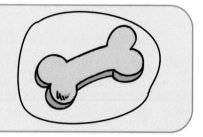

1

2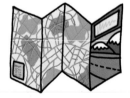

3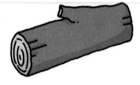

4

Beginning Sounds

▶ **Say the letters in the box. Name each picture. Write the letter that stands for the beginning sound.**

b	h	m	s

Beginning and Ending Sounds

▶ Name each picture. Decide if the name begins or ends with the letter in the box. Write the letter on the correct line.

b

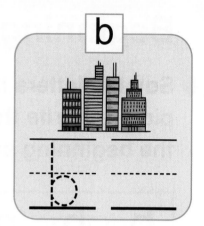

b

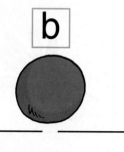

s

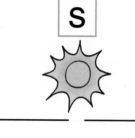

m

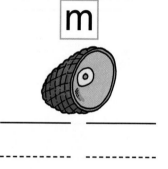

h

s

m

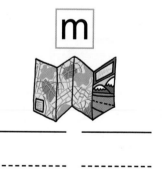

b

h

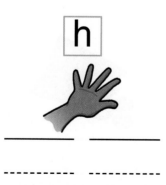

s

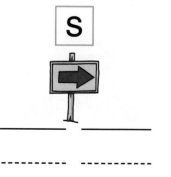

Words to Learn

▶ **Read the words in the box.**
Write the word that belongs
with each picture.

buildings	cars	people	bus

_____

- -

_____

_____

- -

_____

_____

- -

_____

_____

- -

_____

Read Aloud

▶ **Read sentences from "In the City."**
Talk about what you can see
and do in a city.

This is a city.

People work and play here.

They live here, too.

Share

▶ **Draw a picture of another busy place.**
Write a name for your picture.

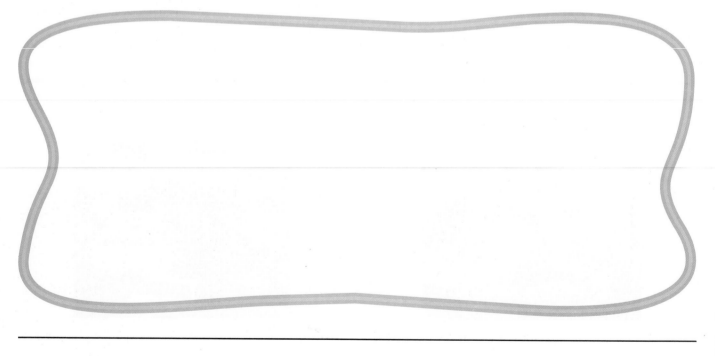

Get Ready to Read
On the Move

1 Topic

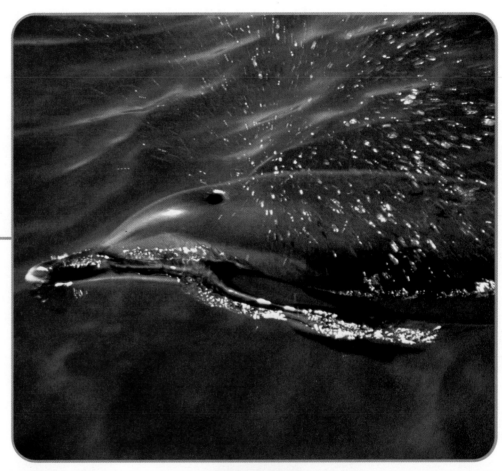

dolphins

2 Words to Learn

dolphins   **sea**   **pod**   **leap**

3 Building Background

What can dolphins do?

On the Move

Dolphins live in the **sea**.
They live in pods.
A **pod** is like a big family.
The dolphins in a pod swim together.

A pod

Dolphins use their tails to move.
Their tails move up and down.
They use their fins to turn and stop.

fin

tail

Dolphins can swim very fast!
They need to catch fish.
They need to get away from sharks.

Dolphins swim and play.
Sometimes they follow ships.
They swim next to the ships
and **leap** out of the water.
They can even walk on their tails!
Dolphins are always on the move.

Tail walking

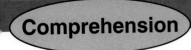

Drawing Conclusions

▶ **Read each sentence. Circle the answer that tells about the sentence.**

1 Dolphins need to catch fish.

Dolphins eat fish.

Dolphins do not eat fish.

2 A pod is like a big family.

There are one or two dolphins in a pod.

There can be many dolphins in a pod.

3 Dolphins swim next to ships.

Dolphins are afraid of ships.

Dolphins are not afraid of ships.

4 Dolphins need to get away from sharks.

Sharks can hurt dolphins.

Sharks can help dolphins.

Beginning Sounds

▶ **Circle the pictures whose names begin
with the same sound.**

1

2

3

4

Beginning Sounds

▶ Say the letters in the box.
Name each picture. Write the letter that
stands for the beginning sound.

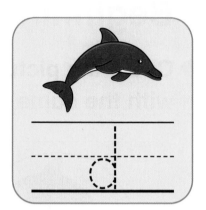

| d | f | g | n |

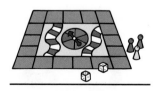

Beginning and Ending Sounds

▶ **Name each picture. Decide if the name begins or ends with the letter in the box. Write the letter on the correct line.**

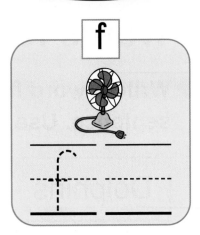

| f |

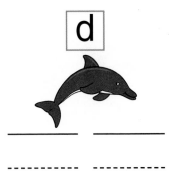

d

f

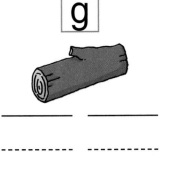

g

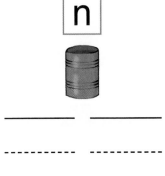

n

d

g

f

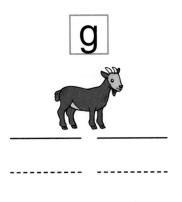

g

d

Words to Learn

▶ **Write a word from the box to finish each sentence. Use the pictures to help you.**

Dolphins	pod	leap	sea

1 Dolphins live in a family

_____

called a _____ .

2 They live in the _____ .

3 _____ swim fast.

4 Dolphins _____

out of the water.

Read Aloud

▶ **Read aloud each sentence. Your partner will echo you.**

Dolphins swim and play.

Sometimes they follow ships.

They swim next to the ships

and leap out of the water.

They can even walk on their tails!

Dolphins are always on the move.

Share

▶ **Draw one thing a dolphin can do. Write about your picture.**

4

Get Ready to Read
Jill and the Jumping Beans

1 **Characters**

Jill

the giant

Jill's family

2 **Setting**

Jill's house

3 **Words to Learn**

jumping beans

beanstalk

giant

golden

4 **Building Background**

What do you know about the story "Jack and the Beanstalk"?

Jill and the Jumping Beans

One day, Jill went for a walk.
She found some **jumping beans**.
Jill's family did not need jumping beans.
They needed money for food.
Jill's family was not happy.

Jill liked the jumping beans.
But they danced away.
Jill ran after them.
The beans went up the **beanstalk**.
So did Jill.

When Jill got to the top, she saw a **giant**.
The giant had the jumping beans.
They made him smile.
Jill asked the giant to give the jumping beans back.
But the giant was lonely.
He wanted to keep the beans.

The giant got a **golden** egg.
He gave the egg to Jill.
Jill let the giant keep the
jumping beans.
The giant was happy!
Jill's family was happy!

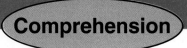

Real and Make-Believe

▶ Draw a picture of something from the story that could not happen in real life. Write about your picture.

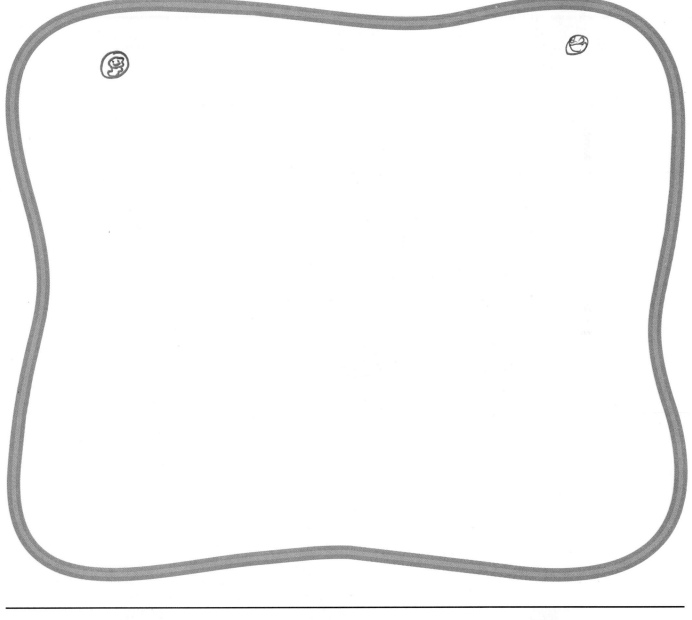

_____

- -

_____

Beginning Sounds

▶ **Circle the pictures whose names begin
with the same sound.**

 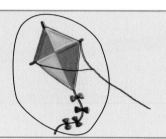 

1

2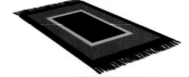

3

4

Beginning Sounds

▶ Circle the pictures whose names begin
with the same sound.

 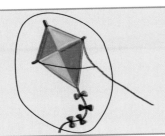 

1

2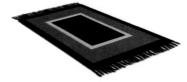

3

4

Real and Make-Believe

▶ Draw a picture of something from the story that could not happen in real life. Write about your picture.

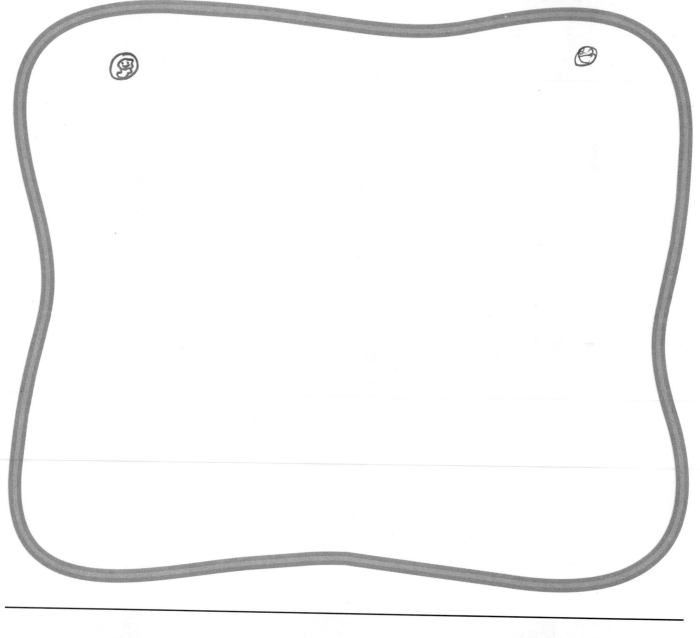

_____

- -

_____

Beginning Sounds

▶ Say the letters in the box. Name each picture. Write the letter that stands for the beginning sound.

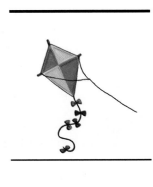

j   k   r   v

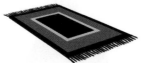

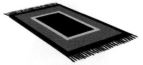

Beginning and Ending Sounds

Name each picture. Decide if the name begins or ends with the letter in the box. Write the letter on the correct line.

k

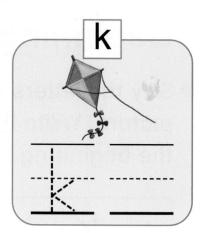

j

k

v

r

v

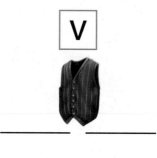

j

k

v

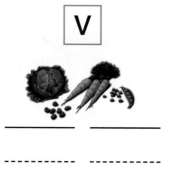

r

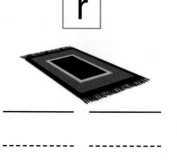

Words to Learn

▶ **Write a word from the box to make each sentence tell about the picture.**

| giant | beanstalk | golden | jumping beans |

1 Jill found some _____.

2 Jill went up the _____ after the beans.

3 The _____ smiled at the beans.

4 The giant gave Jill a _____ egg.

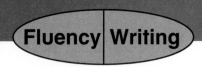
Read Aloud

▶ **Read from the story.**
Take turns with a friend.

The giant got a golden egg.

He gave the egg to Jill.

Jill let the giant keep the

jumping beans.

The giant was happy!

Jill's family was happy!

Share

▶ **Draw a picture of your favorite**
part of the story. Write about it.

Get Ready to Read
Busy As a Bee

1 **Topic**

bees

2 **Words to Learn**

bees   hive   queen   honey

3 **Building Background**

What do you know about bees?

Busy As a Bee

Bees have six legs.
They have four wings.
Bees live in **hives**.
Bees are always busy.

A hive

leg

wings

A queen bee

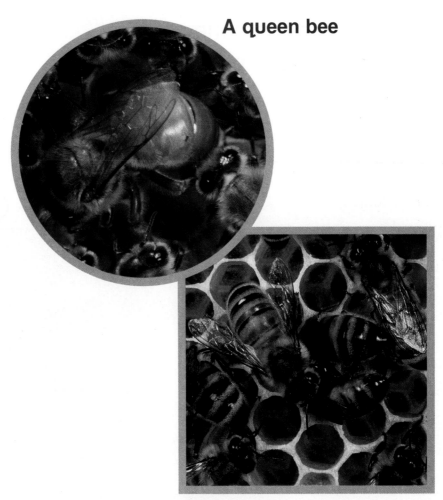

Some worker bees

Bees work together.
The **queen** bee lays eggs.
Worker bees clean the hive.
They keep the hive safe.

Bees make **honey**.
We eat the honey
that bees make.

Getting honey

Wax

Bees make wax, too.
We use the wax
that bees make.
Bees are always busy.

**A candle made
from beeswax**

Classifying

► Fill in the circles with words about bees.

Words About Bees

honey

Beginning Sounds

▶ Circle the pictures whose names begin
with the same sound.

1

2

3

4

Beginning Sounds

▶ Say the letters in the box. Name each picture. Write the letter that stands for the beginning sound.

| qu | w | x | y | z |

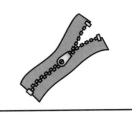

Beginning and Ending Sounds

▶ Name each picture. Decide if the name begins or ends with the letter in the box. Write the letter on the correct line.

X

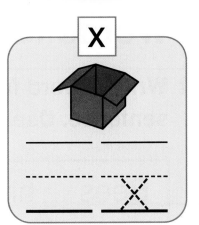

—— ——

- - - - - - - - - X - - - - - -

—— X ——

| qu | x | y |

| z | w | x |

| qu | z | w |

Words to Learn

▶ **Write a word from the box to finish each sentence. Use the pictures to help you.**

Bees	hive	queen	honey

1 Bees live in a _____ .

2 Bees make _____ .

3 The _____ bee lays eggs.

4 _____ are always busy.

Read Aloud

▶ **Read aloud each sentence. Your partner will read the sentence back to you.**

Bees have six legs.
They have four wings.
Bees live in hives.
Bees are always busy.

Share

▶ **Draw a busy bee. Write about your picture.**

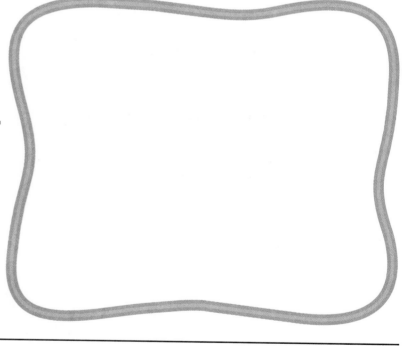

Get Ready to Read
Anna's Rainy Day Song

1 Characters

Anna **Dad** **Mark**

2 Setting

home

3 Words to Learn

rainy **window** **keys** **drum**

4 Building Background

What can you do on a rainy day?

Anna's Rainy Day Song

Anna wants to go to the park.
But today is a **rainy** day.
What can Anna do on this rainy day?

Anna asks Dad to play.
Dad is busy.
He is doing his work.
Anna asks Mark to play.
Mark is busy, too.

Tip, tap goes the rain on the **window**.
Click, clack go Dad's fingers on the **keys**.
POP goes Mark's funny toy.
Anna has an idea!
She gets her **drum**.

"I hear a song," Anna says.

Tip, tap! Click, clack! Rat-a-tat! POP!

"Yes," says Dad. "I can hear your rainy day song."

"Me too!" says Mark.

Anna is happy that today is a rainy day.

Tell the Order

▶ **Finish each sentence.**
Use the words in each box.

| asks Dad and Mark to play. | wants to go to the park. | is happy. |

Beginning

Anna

Middle

Anna

End

Anna

Short *a* Sound

Circle the two pictures in each row that
have the **short a** sound.

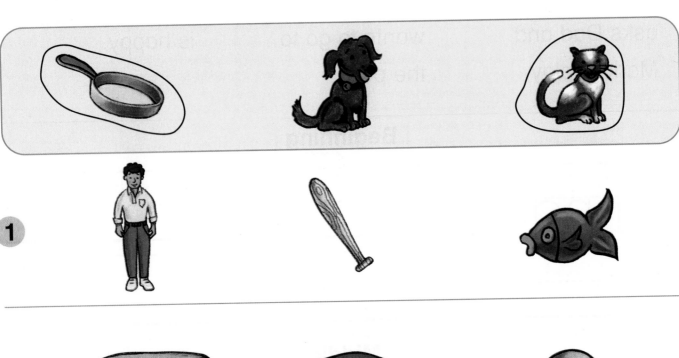

1

2

3

4

Short *a*

▶ **Name each picture. Write** a **if you hear the short** a **sound.**

f a n

v __ n

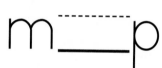

m __ p

b __ s

c __ p

s __ n

p __ n

h __ m

b __ g

d __ g

Short *a*

▶ **Color the pieces that have a short a word.**

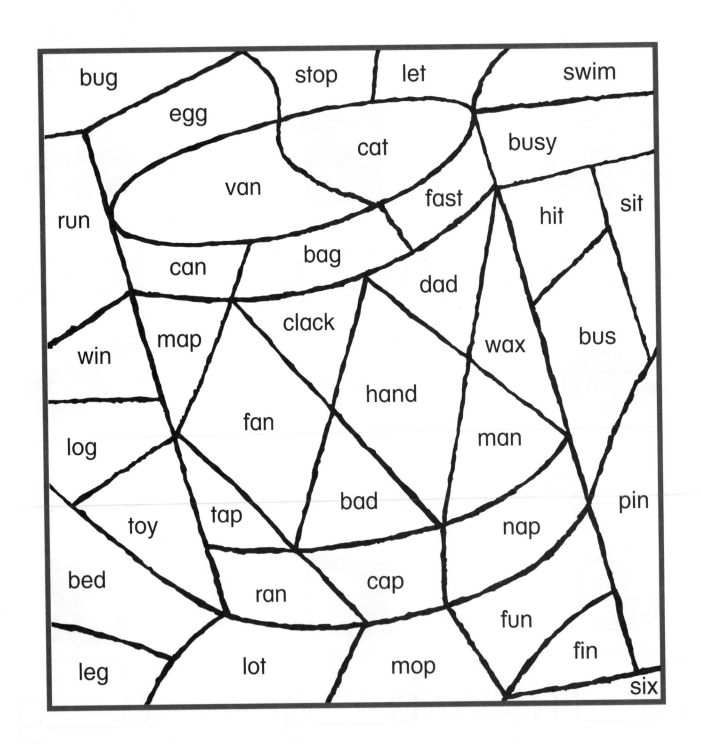

bug

stop

let

swim

egg

cat

busy

van

fast

sit

run

hit

can

bag

dad

map

clack

wax

bus

win

hand

man

fan

log

bad

pin

toy

tap

nap

bed

cap

ran

fun

fin

leg

lot

mop

six

Words to Learn

▶ **Write the word that belongs with each group.**

 rainy    keys    window    drum

_____

1 door, wall, _____

2 song, music, _____

3 windy, cloudy, _____

4 work, fingers, _____

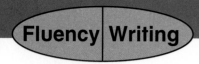

Read Aloud

▶ **Read sentences from the story. Make each word in color sound like the thing it names.**

"I hear a song," Anna says.

Tip, tap! Click, clack! Rat-a-tat! POP!

"Yes," says Dad. "I can hear your rainy day song."

"Me too!" says Mark.

Anna is happy that today is a rainy day.

Share

▶ **What would you do on a rainy day? Write about it.**

_____'s Rainy Day

Get Ready to Read
Let's Go!

1 Topic

getting around

2 Words to Learn

bike

helmet

hike

path

3 Building Background

Do you like to walk or ride a bike?

Let's Go!

We like to ride our **bikes**.
We put on our **helmets**.
We want to be safe.

Now we are ready to go.
We ride like the wind.
We get there fast.

We like to walk.
We **hike** on the **path**.
We stop and we look.
We take our time.

We can go fast.
We can go slow.
Fast or slow, we get
where we want to go.

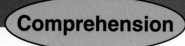

Same and Different

▶ **Circle the answer for each riddle.**

walk   ride

1 You use your feet.

walk   ride   walk and ride

2 You must put on a helmet.

walk   ride   walk and ride

3 You hike on the path.

walk   ride   walk and ride

4 You get where you want to go.

walk   ride   walk and ride

Short *e* Sound

▶ Say each picture name. Circle the pictures whose names have the short e sound.

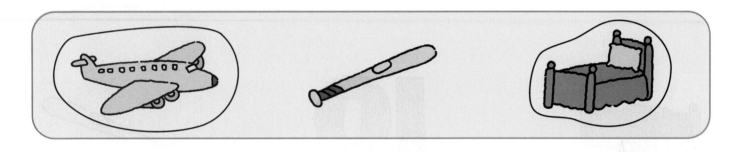

1

2

3

Short *e*

▶ **Name each picture. Write e if you hear the short e sound. Then read the word.**

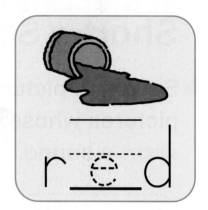

r e d

  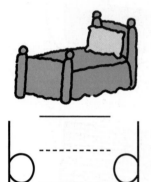

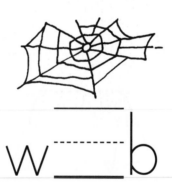 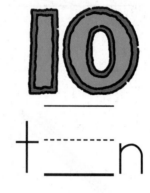

b __ d

t __ n

b __ t

p __ n

w __ b

h __ n

n __ t

j __ t

p __ n

Short *e*

▶ Circle each object whose name has the **short e** sound.

Words to Learn

▶ **Write a word from the box to answer each riddle.**

helmet	bike	path	hike

1 I mean the same as walk.
What am I?

_____

2 You can walk on me.
I rhyme with math.
What am I?

_____

3 I keep your head safe.
What am I?

_____

4 You can ride on me.
I rhyme with like.
What am I?

_____

Read Aloud

▶ **Take turns reading with a partner.**

We can go fast.

We can go slow.

Fast or slow, we get where we want to go.

Share

▶ **How do you like to get where you want to go? Draw a picture and write about it.**

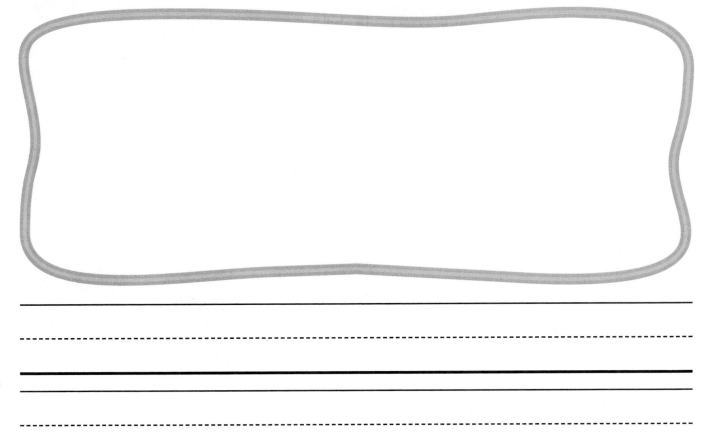

Get Ready to Read
Red Beans and Rice

1 **Characters**

Rick

Grandma

Grandpa

2 **Setting**

Grandma and Grandpa's house

3 **Words to Learn**

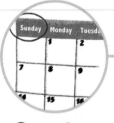
Sunday

dinner

grins

taste

4 **Building Background**

What are your favorite foods?

Red Beans and Rice

Every **Sunday**, we visit Grandma
and Grandpa.
Grandma makes fish for **dinner**.
I love fish!
I always wish for a dish of fish.

Oh, no! What is this?
Grandpa is making dinner this Sunday.
He is not making fish!
I do not like to try new foods.
Oh, I wish for a dish of fish!

Grandpa **grins**.

"Rick, try some red beans and rice.
They are good for you."

But I do not want red beans and rice.
A dish of fish would be so nice!

Grandpa says, "Just try one bite."
Well, maybe I could eat just one.
It isn't bad.
I try some more.
It DOES **taste** good!
Now I WANT red beans and rice.
Trying new foods is very nice!

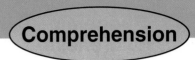

Characters

▶ **Look at the pictures of Rick. Finish the
sentence next to each picture to tell
how Rick changed in the story.**

1 At the beginning of the story,

_____

Rick _____

_____

_____ .

2 At the end of the story,

_____

Rick _____

_____

_____ .

Short *i* Sound

▶ Name each picture. Draw a line from the  to the pictures with the same middle sound.

Short *i*

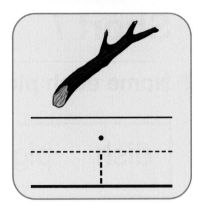

▶ **Name each picture. Write i if you hear the short i sound.**

_____
- - - - - - - - - - - -
_____

_____
- - - - - - - - - - - -
_____

_____
- - - - - - - - - - - -
_____

_____
- - - - - - - - - - - -
_____

_____
- - - - - - - - - - - -
_____

_____
- - - - - - - - - - - -
_____

_____
- - - - - - - - - - - -
_____

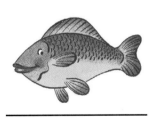
_____
- - - - - - - - - - - -
_____

_____
- - - - - - - - - - - -
_____

Short *i*

▶ **Name each picture. Write the word.**

dish	pig	fish	wig	bib	six

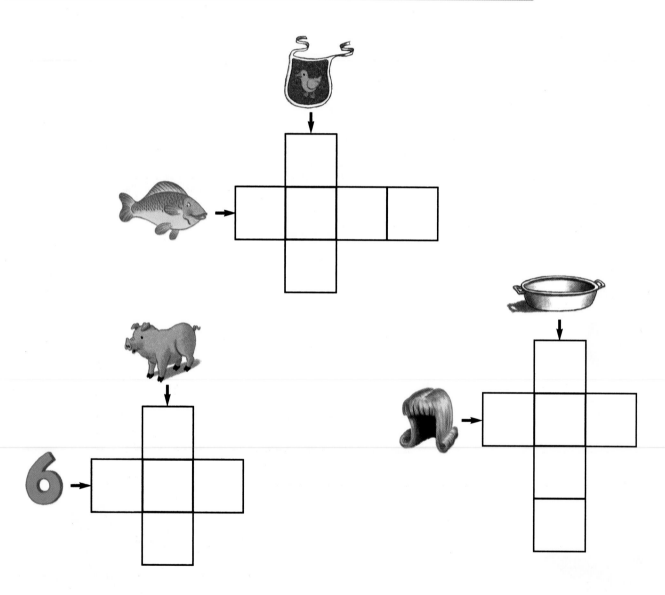

What letter is in every word? _____

Words to Learn

▶ **Write a sentence about each picture.**
Use the word in each sentence.

1 Sunday

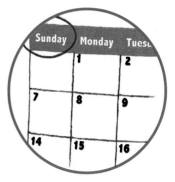

_____

- -

_____

2 dinner

_____

- -

_____

3 grins

_____

- -

_____

4 taste

_____

- -

_____

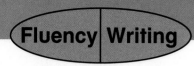

Read Aloud

▶ **Take turns reading sentences from
the story.**

Oh, no! What is this?

Grandpa is making dinner this Sunday.

He is not making fish!

I do not like to try new foods.

Oh, I wish for a dish of fish!

Share

▶ **Write about a new food you learned
to like. Tell why you like it.**

_____

- -

_____

_____

- -

_____

_____

- -

_____

Get Ready to Read
While You Sleep

1 Topic

night workers

2 Words to Learn

team

bakers

doctors

hospital

3 Building Background

What night jobs do you know about?

While You Sleep

The sun goes down.
It is night.
You go to sleep.
But some people go to work.
They have jobs to do at night.

A city at night

While you sleep, a road **team**
goes to work.
They build and fix the roads.
They work at night because there
are not many cars on the road.

A team fixing a road

Bakers making pies

While you sleep, **bakers** go to work.
They make bread for people to buy.
They work at night because people
buy the bread in the morning.

While you sleep, some **doctors**
go to work.
They help sick people in **hospitals**.
Doctors work at night because sick
people need their help.

Doctors at work

The sun comes up.
It is day.
You wake up.
Night workers go to sleep.
The busy night ends.
Now a busy day can start.

Workers starting their day

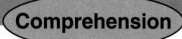
Cause and Effect

▶ **Finish each sentence to tell why some people work at night.**

What Happens   **Why**

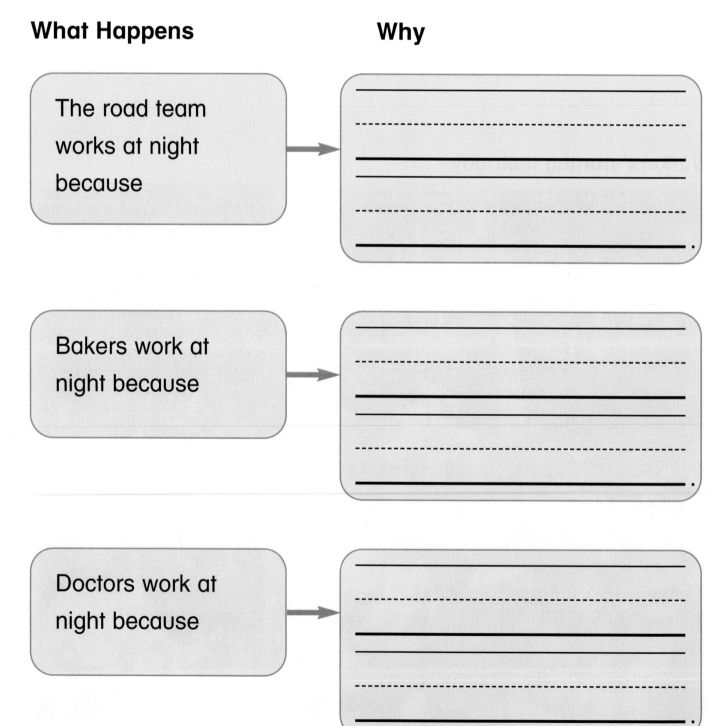

The road team works at night because

Bakers work at night because

Doctors work at night because

Short *o* Sound

▶ Say each picture name. Circle the pictures whose names have the short o sound.

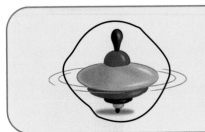  

1

2

3

Short *o*

▶ **Name each picture. Write o if you hear the short o sound. Then say the word.**

d__g

m__p

t__n

b__x

f__x

c__t

b__g

p__g

t__p

l__g

Short *o*

▶ **Write two short o words from the box to describe each picture.**

top	dog	box	hot	pot
log	fox	mop	hops	cot

1 The boy _____ over a _____ .

2 The _____ has a red _____ .

3 A _____ _____ sits in the sun.

4 The _____ has a _____ .

5 The _____ is on the _____ .

Words to Learn

▶ **Use a word from the box to finish each sentence.**

Doctors	bakers	team	hospital

1 At night, workers in the _____ help sick people.

2 They work as a _____ to take care of everyone.

3 _____ help people who are sick or hurt.

4 In hospitals, _____ make food for everyone to eat.

Read Aloud

▶ **Read aloud each sentence.
Your partner will echo you.**

The sun goes down.

It is night.

You go to sleep.

But some people go to work.

They have jobs to do at night.

Share

▶ **Write what you learned about night jobs.**

_____

- -

_____

- -

_____

- -

_____

Get Ready to Read
The Lunch Bunch

1 Characters

**Mandy
Moose**

**Flora
Fox**

**Chipper
Chipmunk**

2 Setting

the forest

3 Words to
Learn

chipmunk

lunch

search

sandwich

4 Building
Background

What do you and your friends like to do at lunchtime?

The Lunch Bunch

Mandy Moose, Flora Fox, and
Chipper **Chipmunk** have **lunch**
together every day.
They eat the same things every day.

Mandy always eats milk and apples.
Flora always eats bread and jam.
Chipper always eats honey and nuts.

"We need a change," said Chipper.
"Yes, we always eat the same things," said Flora.
"We can bring a surprise for each other!" said Mandy.

"For our next lunch, I'll bring a surprise for Mandy," said Chipper.
"I'll bring Chipper's lunch," Flora said.
"And I'll surprise Flora," added Mandy.

The friends went home to **search** for the surprises.
But they could not decide what to bring.
"I don't know what Mandy will like," said Chipper.
"What should I bring for Chipper?" Flora asked.
"Flora won't eat that!" said Mandy.
None of them could find a good surprise to bring.

The next day, the friends met for lunch.
"Surprise!" they all said.
"Oh, no!" said Chipper.
"These aren't new things."
"This is what we ALWAYS have,"
said Flora.
"Then let's put it all in one big
sandwich!" said Mandy.

"Mmm! This tastes good," said Flora.
Chipper grinned and said, "We should
have this for lunch every day!"

110

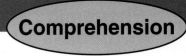

Making Predictions

▶ **The Lunch Bunch also likes to read.
They each read the same book every
day. They need a change. What do you
think they will do? Write about it.**

_____

- -

_____

_____

- -

_____

_____

- -

_____

_____

- -

_____

Short *u* Sound

▶ **Say each picture name. Circle the two pictures in each row that have the short u sound.**

1

2

3

4

Short *u*

▶ **Name each picture. Write u if you hear the short u sound.**

_____

u

_____

suh

_____

dua

_____

fox

_____

_____

_____

_____

_____

B

_____

_____

_____

_____

_____

f

Short *u*

▶ **Say each word. Use the short u words in the box to finish the sentences.**

fun	skip	bus	mud	dirt
bike	moon	sun	sad	run

1 Mandy rides the _____ to school each day.

2 Flora walks to school when the _____ is bright.

3 She walks around the _____ to stay clean.

4 If Chipper is late, then he will _____ to school.

5 The three friends have _____ playing after school.

Words to Learn

▶ **Write a word from the box to finish each sentence. Use the pictures to help you.**

chipmunk	lunch	search	sandwich

1 A _____ is a kind of animal.

2 They ate the same _____ every day!

3 Flora had to _____ for something good to bring.

4 The three friends put all of the foods _____ in a big _____ .

Read Aloud

▶ **Take turns reading sentences from the story.**

The friends went home to search for the surprises.

But they could not decide what to bring.

"I don't know what Mandy will like," said Chipper.

"What should I bring for Chipper?" Flora asked.

"Flora won't eat that!" said Mandy.

None of them could find a good surprise to bring.

Share

▶ **If you were in the Lunch Bunch, what would you bring for lunch? Write about it.**

A Trip to the Zoo

Today we are taking a trip to the zoo.

First, Mom and I get on the bus.

We ride and ride.

The bus stops at the zoo.

We look at many animals.

We see a fish in the water.

We see a bear cub with its mother.

We even spot a zebra.

Next, I get to feed a goat.

Then, it is time to go home.

We have fun at the zoo!

▶ **Read the questions below. Fill in the circle next to the best answer.**

1 Which word starts with the same sound as ?

Ⓐ ride

Ⓑ fun

Ⓒ zoo

Ⓓ bus

2 Which word has the same middle sound as  ?

Ⓐ get

Ⓑ mom

Ⓒ had

Ⓓ cub

3 Which word ends with the same sound as ?

Ⓐ bus

Ⓑ look

Ⓒ get

Ⓓ fun

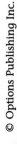

4 What is the story about?

Ⓐ two people going to the zoo

Ⓑ waiting for a bus

Ⓒ two people feeding a goat

Ⓓ a zebra eating lunch

5 What do you know about the girl?

Ⓐ She does not want to ride the bus.

Ⓑ She is scared of the animals.

Ⓒ She has a bad day.

Ⓓ She likes to see animals.

6 What do the girl and Mom do first?

Ⓐ They go home.

Ⓑ They get on the bus.

Ⓒ They see a fish.

Ⓓ They spot a zebra.

7 In this story, what does the word **cub** mean?

Ⓐ a baby bear

Ⓑ a big city

Ⓒ a small home

Ⓓ a park

8 In this story, what does the word **spot** mean?

Ⓐ to see

Ⓑ a place

Ⓒ a dot

Ⓓ to feed

Good work!

Picture Dictionary

Bb

bakers

The <u>bakers</u> made a pie.

beanstalk

A <u>beanstalk</u> is a tall plant.

bees

Honey is made by <u>bees</u>.

bike

She likes to ride her <u>bike</u>.

buildings

The tall <u>buildings</u> are in the city.

bus

We ride the <u>bus</u> to the park.

cars

There are many <u>cars</u> on the street.

chipmunk

A <u>chipmunk</u> is a small animal.

climb

The girl likes to <u>climb</u> things.

Dd

dinner

They ate a big <u>dinner</u>.

doctors

The <u>doctors</u> work at the hospital.

dolphins

The <u>dolphins</u> swim together.

drum

She likes to play her <u>drum</u>.

Ee

eat

They like to <u>eat</u> at the park.

Gg

giant

The <u>giant</u> is very big.

golden

He has a <u>golden</u> egg.

grins

The man <u>grins</u> because he is happy.

 Hh

helmet

I put on my <u>helmet</u> so I do not hurt my head.

hike

He likes to <u>hike</u> in the park.

hive

Bees live in a <u>hive</u>.

124 Picture Dictionary

honey

I like to put <u>honey</u> on my bread.

---

hospital

She went to the <u>hospital</u> because she was sick.

Jj

jumping beans

It is fun to play with <u>jumping beans</u>.

Kk

keys

He tapped the <u>keys</u> with his fingers.

Ll

leap

The dolphin can <u>leap</u> out of the water.

lunch

What will you eat for <u>lunch</u>?

Pp

path

We walked on the <u>path</u>.

people

Many <u>people</u> live in the city.

play

We <u>play</u> ball after school.

pod

A <u>pod</u> is a family of dolphins.

Qq

queen

The <u>queen</u> bee stays in the hive.

Rr

rainy

Today is a <u>rainy</u> day.

run

They <u>run</u> very fast.

Ss

sandwich

I want to eat a <u>sandwich</u>.

sea

The <u>sea</u> is home to many animals.

search

She will <u>search</u> for something to eat.

Sunday

<u>Sunday</u> is a day of the week.

 Tt

---

taste

How does the food <u>taste</u>?

---

team

They work together as a <u>team</u>.

 Ww

---

window

You can look out the <u>window</u>.